Super YC Book's

Dr. Yvonne Chaisson

superycbooks.com

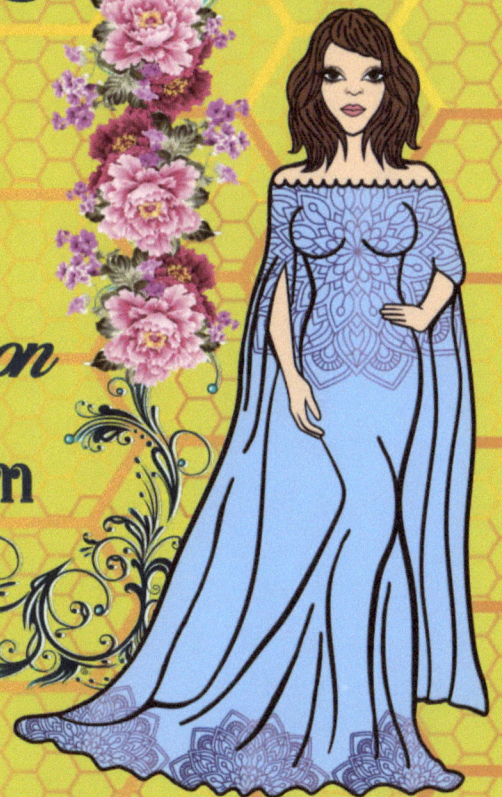

Super YC Book's – The Kings Birthday

Print ISBN   978-0-578-33016-7

Photographer Copyright © 2021
Photographer- Louis Eugene Carpentier

Book Dedication

To my King Grady

This book is for you Happy Birthday

Thank you
For your loving words of Encouragement

For telling me I'm Beautiful

You are my one and only for
35+ Years and counting

I LOVE YOU
Around the World & Back Again
XOXOXOXO

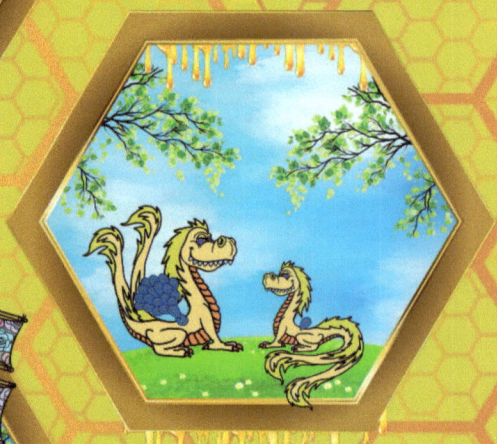

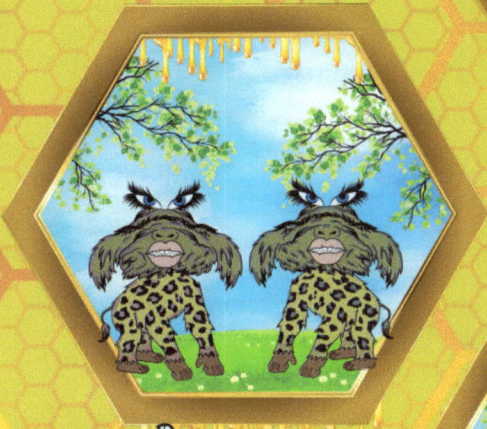

Mr. Bear and Dew Drop
was working hard
collecting all the honey

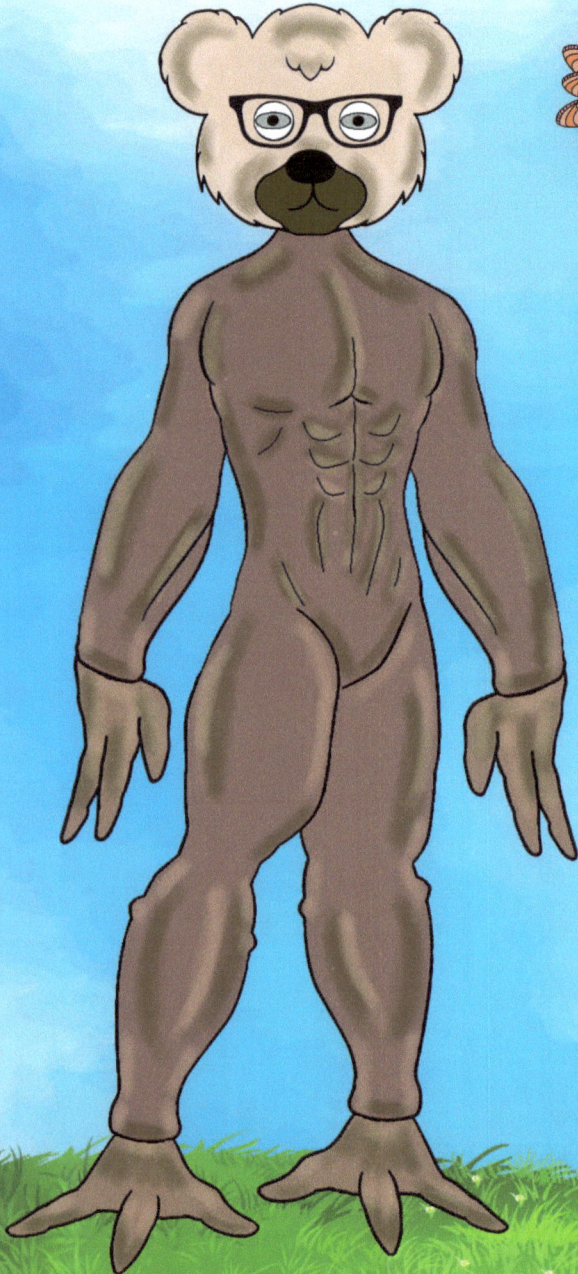

This is the best honey this summer, said Dew Drop

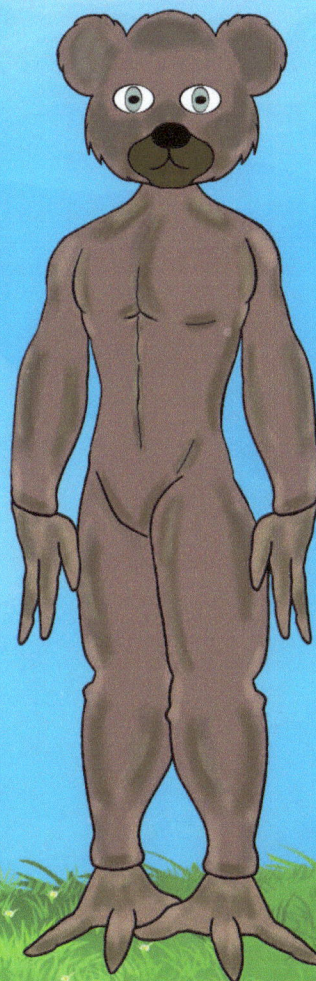

The honey barn is full of honey,
said Dew Drop

Yes, now we need to put up a sign that says
we have honey so everyone knows,
said Mr. Bear

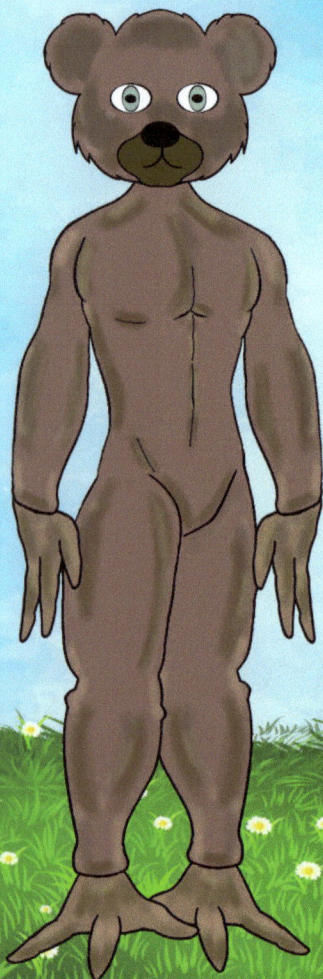

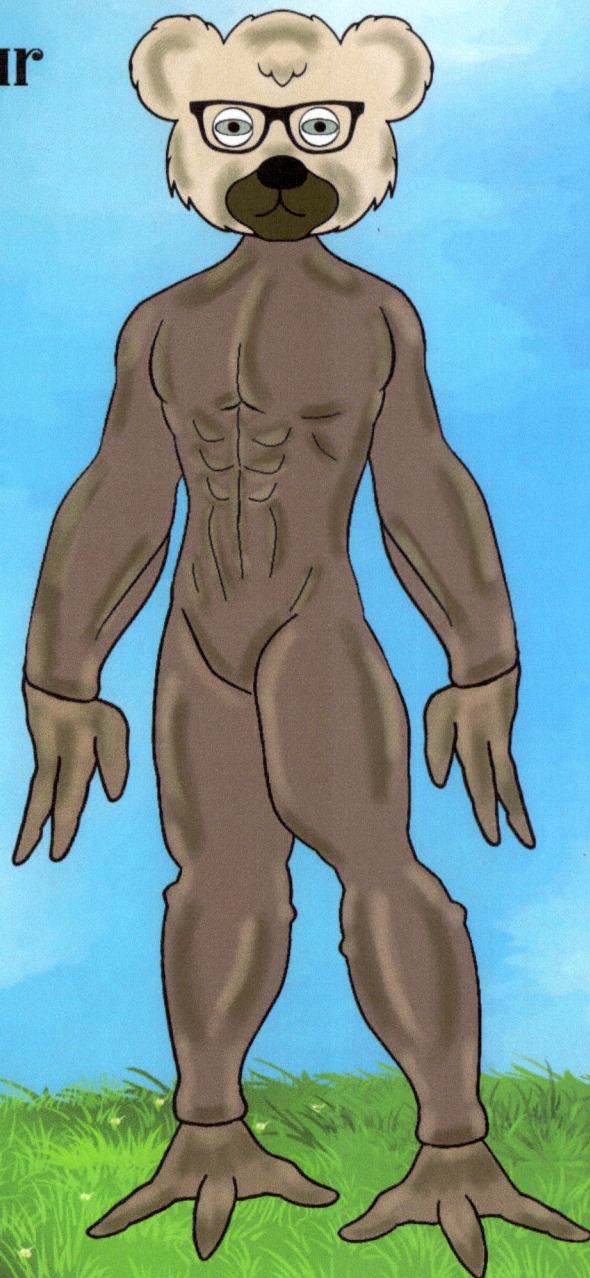

Back at the castle Queen Yvonne asked
Princess Super YC,
Princess Mercy Faith,
and
Princess Charity Rose
to see Mr. Bear,
an ask if the honey is ready for this year

If Mr. Bear has honey
please get three cases of the
absolute best honey
for King Grady's birthday cake,
said Queen Yvonne

Just as they were leaving
Sand Anna ran up to them.
Where are you girls off to? said Sand Anna

To get some honey,
said Princess Super YC

Can I go with you?
I can help you carry the cases of honey
and I also need to get one jar of honey,
said Sand Anna
Yes, you may go with us,
said Princess Mercy Faith

As they were heading to Mr. Bears
they could see from a distance
Mr. Al's and Lilly Bell's
beautiful apple trees full of apples

As they were getting closer
to the apple trees,
they were starting to get hungry

So, they stopped at
the beautiful apple trees
and each of them picked a delicious
looking apple off the tree
to eat along the way

Then off they went
to get the honey at Mr. Bear's

As they came up to Mr. Bear's he was
putting up his sign that said
We Have Honey
Hello girls!!!! said Mr. Bear
how can I help you?

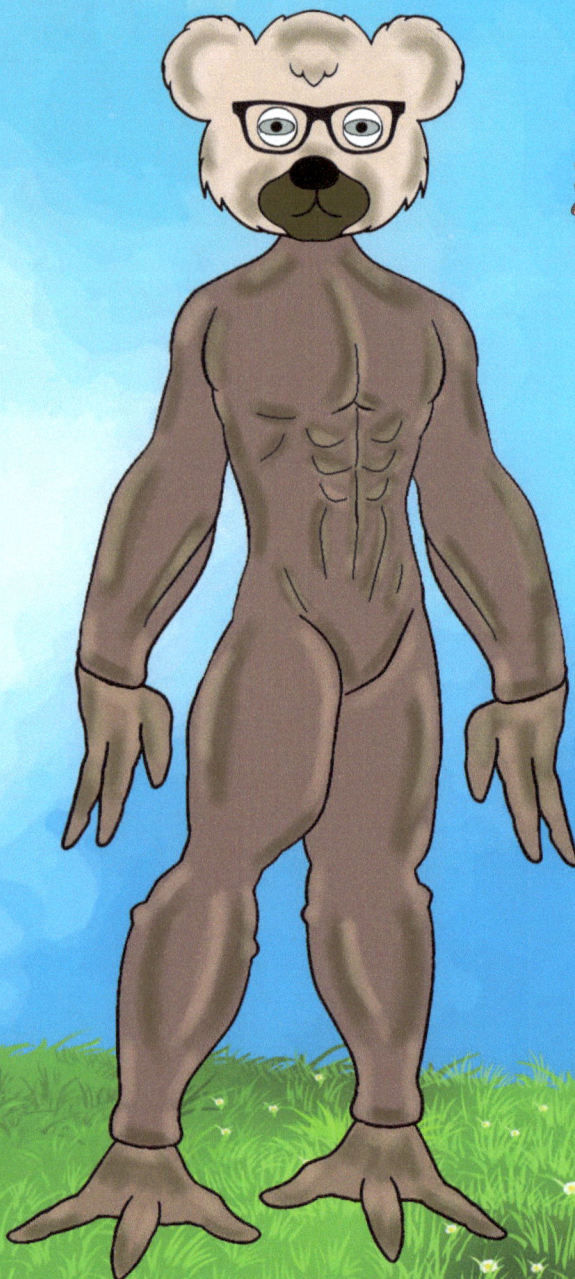

We Have Honey

We have come to see about getting three cases of your absolute best of your honey, said Princess Super YC

We have ten wooden crates
of honey this year.
This is the absolute best
that we have ever got, said Mr. Bear

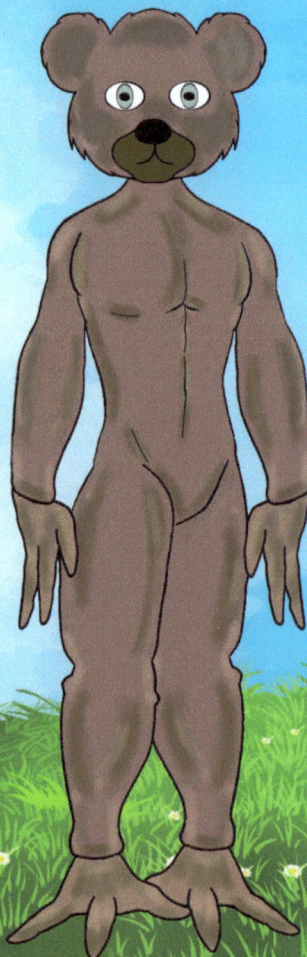

Princess Mercy Faith, Princess Charity Rose,
and Sand Anna each picked
up a case of honey an off they went

As they came by the
Bark of Knowledge Tree, they seen
Violet, Dizzy Daisy,
Flutter Cup, Cornbread all talking,
Is that Mr. Bears honey?
said Bark of Knowledge Tree
Yes, said Sand Anna

Can we get a jar of honey Please?
said Dizzy Daisy
Yes, you can! said Sand Anna
She got them one jar each an off they went

They came by Mr. Al's and Lilly Bell's
they got some more apples
to make their pies and gave
Mr. Al and Lilly Bell each a jar of honey

Then they were on their way home

They saw Popsicle collecting fresh vegetables from his garden, can we please get some of your fresh vegetables? said Princess Super YC

Yes, you can have as much as you want, said Popsicle

Can I have one
jar of the honey please?

Yes, said Princess Super YC

The twins gave him one jar
of honey and got their vegetables.
Then they were on their way to the castle

As they were passing the pond, they saw
Sweetgum, Sourwood, Wildflower,
Star light and Shimmer Playing.
Do you want to play? they asked
Not now we have to get home,
said Princess Super YC

Is that honey from Mr. Bear's?
Can we get a jar each of honey please?
they asked
Yes, you can! so Princess Super YC
gave them each one jar

As they all were approaching the castle gates
Sand Anna said 1 must go home,
but 1 forgot to get one jar of honey
from Mr. Bear
Can 1 have one jar of honey please?

Yes, you can! said Princess Super YC
so Sand Anna took one jar of honey
and headed off for her home
Then they headed towards the castle.

As they came to the castle gates,
Dotted Darnell was guarding
the gates and asked is that
Mr. Bears honey?
Yes, said Princess Mercy Faith

Can I get one jar of honey
please to go with my supper?

Yes, said Princess Charity Rose

They gave Dotted Darnell one jar of honey

When they got to the castle,
Queen Yvonne was waiting for them,
did you get the honey for
King Grady's Birthday cake?
said Queen Yvonne

Yes, we did, and
Mr. Bear said it was
the absolute best honey this year,
said Princess Mercy Faith
and
Princess Charity Rose

As Queen Yvonne looked in the wooden crates. to her surprise there was Peas, Carrots, Purple Tree Collards, Tomatoes, Potatoes, Cabbage and Apples. Where did you get all of this from, said Queen Yvonne?

We got all this from the farmers
along the way home,
we gave them each a jar of
honey to thank them,
said Super YC

Did you forget to keep me one jar of honey to make King Grady's Birthday cake said Queen Yvonne?

Oh No!!!!
We must have given
all the honey away
said Princess Super YC.

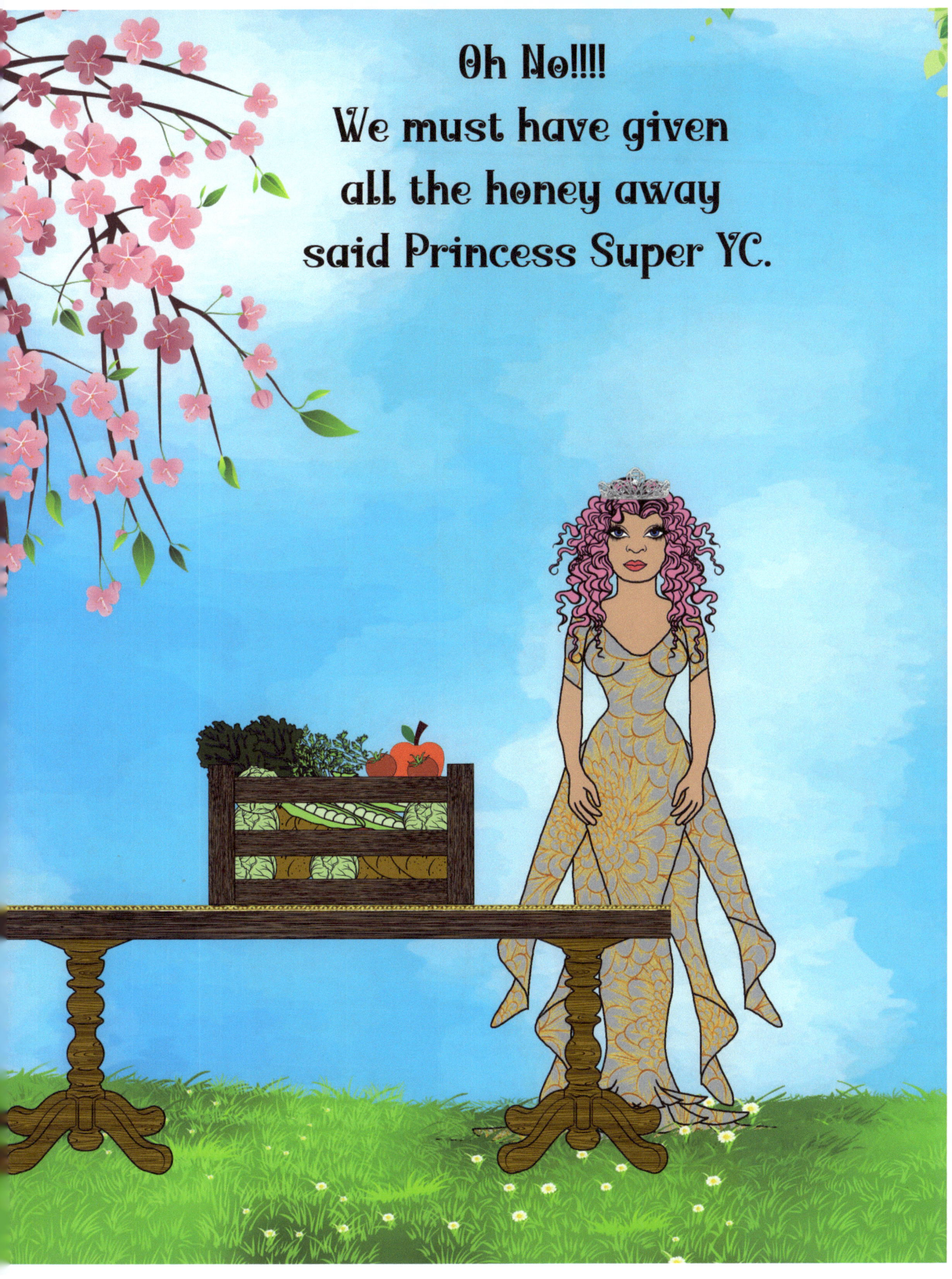

What will we do now!!
We don't even have one jar of
honey to make King Grady's
birthday cake for tomorrow,
said Queen Yvonne

You can have the jar of honey that
the twins gave me to go with
my supper tonight
said Dotted Darnell!!

Mr. Al and Lilly Bell
came to see me today and
said that they know that
Princess Mercy Faith and
Princess Charity Rose
would give away all the
honey on their way home
to all their friends, said Mr. Bear

We would not want to miss your
delicious honey cake
that you are making for
King Grady's Birthday
party tomorrow, said Mr. Bear

Thank you, Mr. Bear,
for all the honey!!!
I will make sure that
King Grady knows your kindness,
said Queen Yvonne

Happy

King

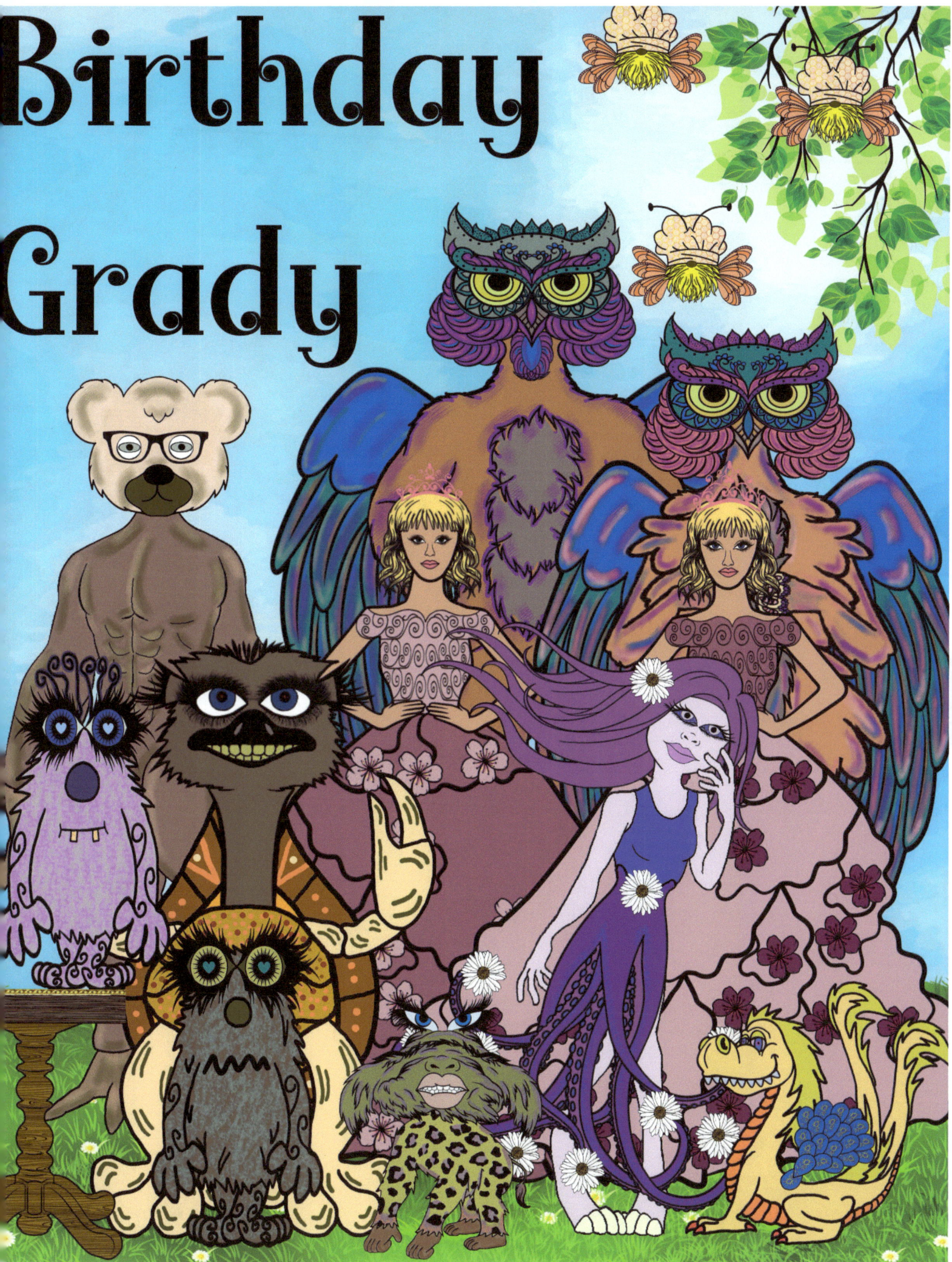

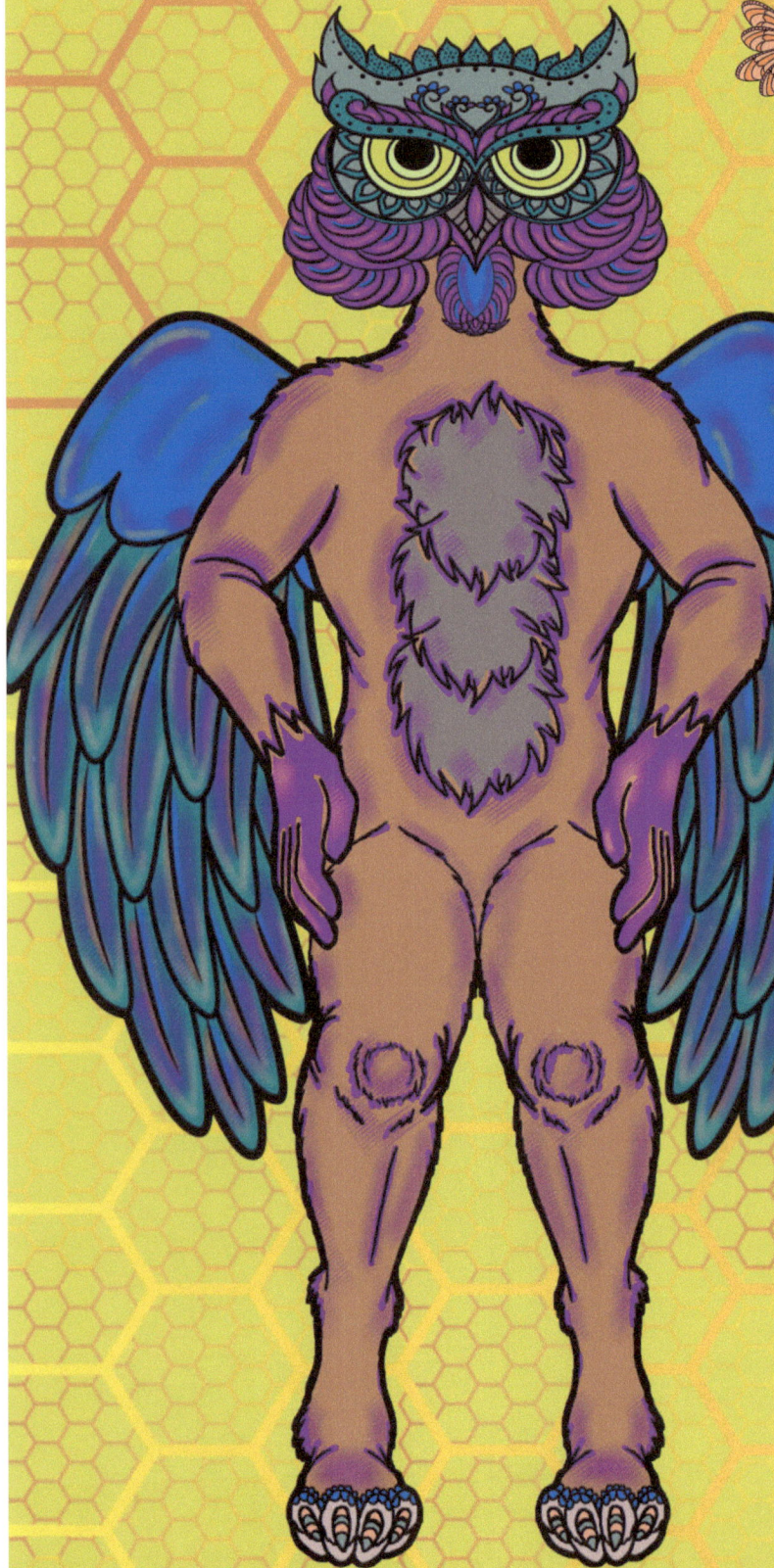

Hey kids!

Did you know that we have 3 Club's?
Official Fan Club
Official Birthday Club
Official Fan Wall Of Art

You can join all our Clubs by sending us a
letter and or a drawing
Please include your name and age,
Your letter or drawing might be featured
in one of our books
We will send you a letter back
with an Awesome Surprise.

Send Letters

Super YC Book's
c/o Yvonne Chaisson
P.O. Box- 211
East Ellijay, Georgia 30539

Official Fan Wall Of Art

Official Art Drawing Contest
Winner and Runner Up
We would like to say Thank You to all the
boys and girls
Who all entered the Drawing Contest at,
Cheeseburger Bobby's in
Canton, Geargia

The Winner
Kadieann Justus Age-1

The Runner-Up
Scarppy Age-61

We would like to say a big Thank You to
Jessica Johnson
for all her help.

Age - 1

Age - 61

Age - 40

Age - 21

Age - 7

Age - 18

Age - 17

Age - 9

Age - 5

Age - 30

Age - 6

Age - 10

Age - 2

Age - 7

My name is Dr. Yvonne Chaisson
I am a proud Published Author & Illustrator of,
Super YC Book's

I am happily married to Grady Chaisson for 35+ years.
Life is at its best.

When I started writing my children's book series,
I would have never imagined that I would become a
World-Renowned Author and Illustrator
winning all the wonderful awards that have been given to me
to have the opportunity to meet all the families and
see how their children have enjoyed my books,
I'm truly Blessed by and appreciate my fans
with my whole heart,
Thank You to all my Fans.

Please
Follow, Like, Share and Subscribe

superycbooks.com

www.facebook.com/Dr.YvonneChaisson

www.facebook.com/SuperYCBooks

YouTube - Super YC Book's

www.ingramcontent.com/pod-product-compliance
Lightning Source LLC
Chambersburg PA
CBHW042017090426

42811CB00015B/1666